D0528495

Christmas Food Made Simple

John Topham

LAMONA & John Topham

The Perfect Combination

John Topham

Christmas food made simple...

This is a busy time of year in most kitchens, so I've put together all my festive favourites to help you enjoy the best of Christmas home cooking. Whether you're feeding the family right through the season, or just entertaining friends with one or two special meals, I hope these dishes will make your celebrations memorable.

You'll discover the secrets to creating some great British classics, plus new ideas to appeal to all tastes. There really is something for everyone.

I've made all the recipes using Lamona appliances, so I'm confident you'll get fantastic results. If you don't normally do a lot of cooking, Christmas is the time to have a go – and if you're more experienced, you'll love spreading the festive cheer at every opportunity.

Whatever kind of cook you are, the Lamona range offers you plenty of choice. And when you're all set up with your new Lamona appliances, what better way to celebrate, than with these festive recipes?

Have a very merry Christmas and a happy New Year!

John Topham

Head Chef and owner, The General Tarleton

LAMONA & John Topham

The Perfect Combination

Starting the Baking Early

Seasonal Extras to Prepare in Advance

Kick-starting the Big Day

Christmas Day Starters

Christmas Day Roast

Desserts for the Perfect Finalé

Seasonal Main Dishes

Making the Most of the Left Overs

Festive Entertaining

Starting the baking early

As Christmas approaches, it's good to get ahead on your baking. As well as saving you time later, the cake and the pudding always taste better when they've had time to mature.

Christmas Pudding and Rum Sauce

Christmas Pudding

Serves 6   20 mins preparation, 4 hours 30 mins cooking (2 hours 30 mins reheating)

Ingredients

2 eggs

1 pinch mixed spice

¼ teaspoon grated nutmeg

½ teaspoon ground cinnamon

1 pinch salt

50ml Armagnac (or brandy)

½ orange – juice and grated zest

½ lemon – juice and grated zest

100g brown sugar

100g raisins

100g currants

100g sultanas

100g breadcrumbs

75g suet

40g almonds, blanched and roughly chopped

½ Bramley cooking apple

50g mixed peel

40g self-raising flour

1½ pint pudding basin, greased and lined with greaseproof paper

1. In a small bowl, lightly beat the eggs, then add the mixed spice, nutmeg, cinnamon, salt, Armagnac, orange and lemon juice and zest. Whisk to combine.

2. In a large bowl, mix all the other ingredients, followed by the egg and spice mixture. Mix thoroughly and pack into the pudding basin. Cover with a circle of greaseproof paper and a double layer of foil on top, then tie securely with string.

3. Place the pudding into a steamer, and steam for 4½ hours. Keep checking the water level and top up as necessary with boiling water.

4. Remove the pudding from the steamer and leave to cool. When it's cold, take off the foil lid and replace with cling film. Store in a cool place until you need it on Christmas Day. (It will keep for up to 2 months).

5. To reheat the pudding on the day, steam it for a further 2½ hours.

Rum Sauce

Serves 4-6   20 mins preparation and cooking

Ingredients

40g unsalted butter at room temperature

40g plain flour

570ml milk

50g caster sugar

4-5 tablespoons dark rum

1. Using your hands, cream the butter and flour into a smooth paste. This takes about 3-5 minutes of kneading.

2. In a small saucepan, heat the milk to simmering point.

3. Turn the heat to low, and whisk in the butter and flour paste a little at a time, until the sauce thickens to a nice, pouring consistency.

4. Cook for a further 5 minutes on a low heat, stirring from time to time.

5. Add the sugar and rum to taste. Pour into a jug and keep warm until you need it.

Christmas Cake

Christmas Cake

30 mins preparation, 12 hours soaking, 3 hours 30 mins cooking

Ingredients

400g currants

200g sultanas

200g raisins

150g glacé cherries, roughly chopped

50g mixed peel

4 tablespoons Armagnac (or brandy)

225g plain flour

½ teaspoon salt

½ teaspoon cinnamon

½ teaspoon mixed spice

¼ teaspoon ground nutmeg

225g unsalted butter

225g soft brown sugar

1 dessert spoon black treacle

4 eggs, beaten

50g almonds, chopped

Zest of 1 lemon

Zest of 1 orange

20cm round cake tin

1. At least 12 hours before you're ready to start baking, soak the currants, sultanas, raisins, cherries and mixed peel in the Armagnac in a covered bowl.

2. Line a 20cm round cake tin with greaseproof paper, so that both sides and base are covered. Place a piece of double thickness brown paper around the outside of the tin and secure with string. This is to stop the outside of the cake over-cooking during the long cooking process.

3. Preheat the oven to 140°C/gas mark 1, and place the shelf as low down as possible.

4. Sift the flour and spices into a bowl.

5. Using an electric mixer, in a separate bowl beat the butter, sugar and treacle. Then slowly add the beaten eggs, a little at a time, beating thoroughly after each addition. Once they are fully mixed in, turn the mixer off and add the spiced flour, chopped almonds, and orange and lemon zest. With the mixer set at its lowest, continue to mix until all the ingredients are combined.

6. Fold in the soaked fruit, then transfer the cake mixture to the prepared cake tin. Cover with a layer of greaseproof paper.

7. Bake for 3½ hours. To test the cake is cooked, insert a skewer or thin-bladed knife into the centre of the cake. If it comes out clean, the cake is ready – it should feel firm when you touch the top, but not be too browned.

8. Leave to cool for half an hour, then remove from the cake tin and place on a wire rack to cool fully. Once it's cold, wrap in a double layer of greaseproof paper, followed by a double layer of tin foil. Keep in an airtight container until you need it, for up to 8 weeks.

Icing the cake

I think life's too short (or too busy) to make your own marzipan and icing – and for me, the cake itself is the main event. Having said that, in my house the children love the marzipan and icing, and decorating the cake is as much a part of my daughter Phoebe's Christmas as decorating the tree. So I always buy the best marzipan and ready-to-roll icing, and I suggest you do the same – from a good cake ingredients shop or on the internet, 500g of each will be enough to ice the cake.

Mince Pies

Right through the Christmas season, it's always good to have mince pies at the ready. I love this almond and orange pastry – it gives an extra dimension to the sweet festive flavours.

Makes 18 pies 25 mins preparation, 20 mins cooking, 1 hour chilling

Ingredients

75g icing sugar, plus extra for dusting

150g unsalted butter at room temperature, plus extra for greasing pie tray

1 egg, beaten

½ orange – juice and grated zest

250g plain flour, plus extra for rolling pastry

1 pinch salt

25g ground almonds

400g jar of good quality mincemeat

2 tablespoons milk

7.5cm fluted pastry cutter

6cm fluted pastry cutter

Pie tray

1. Preheat the oven to 190°C/gas mark 5.

2. Using an electric mixer, blend the sugar and butter until light and fluffy. Then slowly add the beaten egg, a little at a time, followed by the orange juice and zest.

3. Sieve the flour into a separate bowl, add the salt and ground almonds, and mix together. With the mixer on a low speed, gradually add the flour mixture to the sugar and butter mixture to form a soft dough.

4. Wrap the dough in cling film and chill in the fridge for 1 hour.

5. Roll out the dough on a cool, lightly floured work surface until 3mm thick. Use a 7.5cm fluted pastry cutter to cut out 12 bases, and a 6cm fluted pastry cutter to make 12 lids. (You'll have enough for 6 more – see step 8 below.)

6. Lightly grease a mince pie tray with the extra butter. Place the pastry bases into the tray and fill each one with a teaspoon of mincemeat, being careful not to overfill. Using a pastry brush dipped in milk, dampen the edges of the pastry lids, then place onto the filled pies and gently press to seal. Brush the surfaces with a little more milk and use scissors to make a small slit in the centre of each pie.

7. Bake for 20 minutes, until golden. Leave to cool in the tray for 5 minutes, then remove and place on a wire rack to cool fully.

8. When the mince pie tray has cooled, make the remaining 6 pies.

9. Dust with icing sugar to serve.

Mince Pies

Christmas Tree Biscuits

Christmas Tree Biscuits

If you like to make your own Christmas decorations, try these edible ones.
They look good, and taste even better!

Makes 24 biscuits (approx.)   **30 mins preparation, 15 mins cooking**
15 mins icing, 1 hour 20 mins chilling

Ingredients

275g plain flour, plus extra for rolling

1 pinch salt

½ teaspoon baking powder

¼ teaspoon ground cloves

1 teaspoon ground cinnamon

110g unsalted butter

185g caster sugar

1 egg

1 teaspoon lemon juice

Zest of ½ lemon

For the icing:

1 egg white

2 tablespoons lemon juice

200g icing sugar

Edible decorations (optional)

Piping bag

Christmas-themed biscuit cutters

1. Preheat the oven to 170°C/gas mark 3.

2. Sift the flour, salt, baking powder, cloves and cinnamon into a bowl.

3. Using an electric mixer, in a separate bowl beat the butter and sugar until light and fluffy.

4. In a separate bowl, whisk the egg. Then slowly add the egg, lemon juice and zest to the butter and sugar mixture.

5. With the mixer on a low speed, gradually add the spiced flour to form a soft dough.

6. Knead on a work surface for 20 seconds, then wrap in cling film and chill in the fridge for at least 1 hour.

7. Roll out the dough on a cool, lightly floured work surface until 3mm thick. Using Christmas-themed biscuit cutters, stamp out your Christmas shapes, then place on a greaseproof-lined baking tray and chill for 20 minutes.

8. Before you cook the biscuits, make a small hole in each one, so you can hang them from your Christmas tree with string or ribbon.

9. Bake the biscuits for 15 minutes, until golden. Leave on the baking sheet for 5 minutes to crispen, then move them onto a wire rack to cool.

To make the icing:

1. Beat the egg white in a bowl, add the lemon juice and gradually stir in the icing sugar until you have a smooth mixture.

2. Spoon the icing into a piping bag and ice your biscuits, adding edible decorations if you wish.

Almond Financiers

You can find these little cakes in some of the finest patisseries in Paris. They are crusty on the outside and moist in the middle – very moreish and a lovely treat for Christmas time.

Makes 36 cakes (approx.) 45 mins preparation, 15 mins cooking

Ingredients

For the syrup:
60g caster sugar
45g glucose
120ml water

For the almond paste:
145g blanched almonds
145g icing sugar
150ml syrup (see above)

For the Financiers:
170g unsalted butter
150g caster sugar
310g almond paste (see left)
3 eggs
1 tablespoon brandy
85g strong plain flour
¼ teaspoon baking powder

2 tablespoons flaked almonds
1 orange – juice and grated zest
1 teaspoon fresh rosemary, finely chopped

Bun tray and paper cases

To make the syrup:

1. Put the caster sugar, glucose and water in a saucepan, bring to the boil and simmer for 2 minutes.

2. Set aside to cool.

To make the almond paste:

1. In a food processor, grind the almonds, then add the icing sugar and blend.

2. Turn the processor to the lowest setting and gradually add 150ml of the syrup, blending into a paste.

To make the Financiers:

1. Preheat the oven to 190°C/gas mark 5.

2. Melt the butter in a small saucepan, then keep on the heat until it goes golden brown. Remove from the heat and leave to cool. This is a 'beurre noisette', French for 'brown butter' (or literally, 'hazelnut butter').

3. Using an electric mixer, blend the sugar and almond paste and gradually add the cooled beurre noisette.

4. Check the mixing bowl to make sure nothing is sticking, then add the eggs one at a time, making sure each one is mixed in before adding the next.

5. Add the brandy, mix it in, then turn off the mixer.

6. Sift the flour and baking powder, add to the mixing bowl and fold in gently using the lowest mixer speed until smooth.

7. Place the bun cases in the bun tray and spoon in the mixture until they are three quarters full. Sprinkle with flaked almonds and cook for 15 minutes, until golden brown.

8. In a small saucepan, warm the remaining syrup with the orange juice and zest until reduced to a sticky syrup. Add the chopped rosemary and brush onto the Financiers. Best served when still slightly warm.

Almond Financiers

Seasonal extras to prepare in advance

Pickles and chutneys add a lovely traditional character to your Christmas cooking, and making them early really gets you in the festive mood. It's nice to know they're ready and waiting for hungry guests to arrive.

Apple and Vanilla Pickle and Cumberland Sauce

Cumberland Sauce

Makes 2 jars   **30 mins preparation and cooking**

Ingredients

2 oranges

1 lemon

2 shallots, finely chopped

25g fresh ginger root, peeled and grated

150ml port

300g jar of redcurrant jelly

2 teaspoons English mustard powder

1 teaspoon arrowroot

1 teaspoon fresh thyme, chopped

Sterilised jars (approx 454g size)

1. Thinly peel the zest from the oranges and lemon. Remove any pith and cut into thin strips. Blanch in boiling water for 2 minutes, then drain and rinse under cold water.

2. Squeeze the juice from the oranges and lemon, saving 2 tablespoons in a small bowl. Add the rest to a small saucepan, along with the chopped shallots, grated ginger, port and redcurrant jelly. Bring to the boil and simmer gently for 15 minutes. Remove from the heat.

3. Add the mustard powder and arrowroot to the orange and lemon juice you saved. Mix until smooth, then whisk into the jelly mixture until shiny. Stir in the thyme and the blanched orange and lemon zest, then pour into sterilised jars. Keep in a cool place until you need it, for up to 2-3 months.

Apple and Vanilla Pickle

Makes 2 jars   **20 mins preparation, 1 hour cooking**

Ingredients

150g caster sugar

300ml cider vinegar

1 onion, finely chopped

1 vanilla pod, split lengthways

6 Granny Smith apples

80g golden raisins

Sterilised jars (approx 454g size)

1. In a heavy-bottomed pan, dissolve the sugar in the cider vinegar, bring to a simmer, then add the chopped onion and split vanilla pod.

2. Simmer gently while you peel, core and dice the apples into 1cm pieces.

3. Using a whisk, disperse the vanilla seeds from the pod. Then add the chopped apple and raisins and simmer gently for a further 40 minutes.

4. Remove the vanilla pod and pour the pickle into sterilised jars. Keep in a cool place until you need it, for up to 2-3 months.

Christmas Chutney

As its name suggests, this chutney is full of festive flavour, and complements any cold meat or game, cheeses or savoury pies. It also makes a lovely homemade Christmas gift.

Makes 2 jars   **20 mins preparation, 1 hour cooking, 2-3 weeks maturing**

Ingredients

1 onion, finely chopped

400g caster sugar

400ml cider vinegar

300g dried prunes

300g dried dates

300g dried apricots

25g fresh ginger root, peeled and grated

1 teaspoon salt

¼ teaspoon dried chilli flakes

½ cinnamon stick

3 star anise

2 teaspoons mustard seeds

1 orange – juice and grated zest

Sterilised jars (approx 454g size)

1. Add the onion, sugar and vinegar to a heavy-bottomed pan and bring to a simmer.

2. Chop the prunes, dates and apricots into small, evenly sized chunks. Add them to the reducing vinegar along with the rest of the ingredients. Bring back to a simmer, reduce the heat and cook for 1 hour, stirring occasionally.

3. Remove from the heat, then discard the cinnamon stick and star anise. Pour into sterilised jars, seal and store in a cool place.

4. Leave for 2-3 weeks to mature, then keep until you need it, for up to 4 months.

Pickled Cherries

Quick and easy to make, these bitter-sweet cherries work well with almost any cold meat or cheese – and they look very impressive on the plate.

Makes 2 jars   **10 mins preparation and cooking**

Ingredients

24 cherries with stems attached

110ml red wine vinegar

55ml water

60g caster sugar

Sterilised jars (approx 454g size)

1. Place all the ingredients in a saucepan, bring to the boil and simmer for 2 minutes.

2. Pour into sterilised jars. Keep in the fridge until you need it, for up to 2 weeks.

Christmas Chutney and Pickled Cherries

Kick-starting the big day

Breakfast is the most important meal of any day, but on Christmas Day it's vital. You need something to sustain you through an exciting morning — and with these recipes, you'll make it an extra special treat too.

Eggs Benedict

Eggs Benedict

Christmas is a great excuse for an indulgent breakfast, and this will really set you up for the day. Okay, it's quite substantial – but you need something to keep you going until the turkey's ready!

Serves 4   25 mins preparation and cooking

Ingredients
Salt
1 dessert spoon malt vinegar
4 eggs
2 English muffins
25g unsalted butter
4 slices ham

For the Hollandaise Sauce:
120g unsalted butter
2 egg yolks
1 tablespoon white wine vinegar
Salt and milled black pepper
1 pinch paprika
Juice of 1 lemon

To make the Hollandaise Sauce:

1. Start by clarifying the butter. To do this, melt it gently in a pan and scoop off any solids that form on the surface. Carefully ladle the clear melted butter from the milky liquid and keep it to one side until you need it.

2. Add the egg yolks and vinegar to a heat-proof bowl and place over a saucepan of just simmering water. Whisk for 2 minutes, until you can see the trail of your whisk in the mixture.

John's tip: Be very careful not to overheat the eggs, as they can scramble and give you a lumpy sauce. To prevent this, you may need to remove the bowl from the simmering water from time to time.

3. Still whisking, slowly add the clarified butter. When it's all mixed in, remove from the heat and season with salt, pepper, paprika and lemon juice to taste. Keep in a warm place.

To finish the Eggs Benedict:

1. Bring a large saucepan of water to a gentle simmer, then add a pinch of salt and the malt vinegar.

2. Crack each egg into a separate teacup.

3. Using a large spoon, stir the simmering water vigorously so it forms a whirlpool. Gently slide your eggs into the circling water and cook for 2-3 minutes until the whites are set. Using a slotted spoon, carefully remove the eggs from the water and drain on kitchen paper.

4. Slice the muffins in two, then lightly toast and butter them. Place each half on a plate and fold a slice of ham onto each one, followed by a poached egg.

5. Spoon over the Hollandaise Sauce, dust with paprika and serve immediately.

American Pancakes with Crispy Bacon and Maple Syrup

Try these for a different way to serve bacon for breakfast. The sweet syrup and pancakes balance the saltiness beautifully – it's a really satisfying mix of flavours and textures.

Serves 4   20 mins preparation and cooking

Ingredients

2 teaspoons baking powder

¼ teaspoon bicarbonate of soda

150g plain flour

50g caster sugar

25g unsalted butter

2 eggs

150ml buttermilk

12 rashers streaky rindless bacon

Corn or vegetable oil for cooking

4 tablespoons maple syrup

1. Sift the baking powder, bicarbonate of soda and flour into a large bowl and add the sugar.

2. Melt the butter in a saucepan over a low heat, then keep warm.

3. Crack the eggs into a separate bowl and whisk, adding the buttermilk and melted butter. Then pour this into the flour mixture and whisk to a smooth batter with a balloon whisk. At this stage, you can either store the batter in the fridge for a couple of hours or use straight away.

4. When you're ready to cook the pancakes, grill the bacon on both sides until crispy and keep warm.

5. Heat a large frying pan and add a little of the oil. Then, working in batches, drop large tablespoonfuls of the batter into the pan, allowing space in between.

6. Cook for 2 minutes, then flip over using a palette knife. Cook for a further minute, until golden and cooked through. Keep in a warm place while cooking the rest of the pancakes.

7. To assemble the dish, split the pancakes between 4 plates, add 3 rashers of bacon on top and drizzle with maple syrup, and a knob of butter if you wish.

American Pancakes with Crispy Bacon and Maple Syrup

Smoked Salmon and Scrambled Eggs

This combination is welcome at any time of year, but its rich, creamy flavours and textures go down particularly well at a festive breakfast.

Serves 4   15 mins preparation and cooking

Ingredients
8 eggs
Salt and milled black pepper
30g unsalted butter
2 tablespoons milk
4 slices brown toast, buttered
300g smoked salmon, sliced
Fresh chives, chopped

1. Crack the eggs into a bowl. Season with salt and pepper and lightly beat together – just enough to break up the yolks.

2. Melt the butter in a non-stick saucepan on a low heat. Add the milk and beaten eggs and cook for 2-3 minutes, stirring continuously until they are softly scrambled.

3. Serve immediately with the buttered toast. Divide the smoked salmon between the plates, with a twist of black pepper and chives to garnish.

John's tip: The eggs will continue to cook even after you've taken them off the heat. So it's better to under-cook them slightly, rather than risk making them rubbery.

Smoked Salmon and Scrambled Eggs

Festive Five Fruits

If you feel the need for something a little lighter than the traditional Christmas fare, this tropical fruit dish makes a very refreshing change.

Serves 4   15 mins preparation

Ingredients

2 oranges

2 pink grapefruit

1 mango

4 kiwi fruit

2 passion fruit

4 sprigs mint (optional)

1. Peel the oranges and pink grapefruit. To do this, cut off the top and bottom, removing the skin and pith and exposing the flesh. Stand the fruit on one of the cut sides and carefully remove the rest of the skin and pith by slicing from top to bottom, following the curved shape of the fruit with your knife. Work your way around each fruit, until you've removed all the skin and pith.

2. Insert a sharp knife in between each orange and grapefruit segment, removing it from the fruit as you go and leaving the segment membrane behind. Place the segments in a bowl and squeeze over any excess juice from the remains of the fruit.

3. Slice the mango in half, cutting around the large oval stone. Carefully cut each half into quarters lengthways and then run a knife along the skin to remove it. Dice the fruit into chunks and add to the orange and grapefruit segments.

4. Peel the kiwi fruit and cut into small cubes. Add this to the other prepared fruit and divide into 4 bowls.

5. Cut the passion fruit in half across the centre and scoop out the seeds with a teaspoon. Scoop half onto each dish and serve with a sprig of mint.

Christmas Day starters

You'll want to get Christmas lunch off to a flying start. These recipes will help you create the perfect prelude to your roast – in traditional style or with something more adventurous.

Gravadlax

Gravadlax

Originating in Scandinavia, this recipe for cured salmon seems to suit our chilly winter weather. At home, I make it as a change from traditional smoked salmon – everyone loves its distinctive dill flavour.

Serves 4   15 mins preparation, 36 hours curing

Ingredients
2 teaspoons black peppercorns
100g fresh dill
35g demerara sugar
70g sea salt
2 tablespoons whisky
500g salmon fillet (ask your fishmonger for a boned centre piece, with the skin on)

To serve:
50g fresh dill
1 tablespoon olive oil
Pickled beetroot
Creamed horseradish
Brown bread

1. In a warm saucepan, roll and toast the peppercorns for 1 minute, then crush them lightly in a pestle and mortar.

2. Chop the dill very finely and mix in a bowl with the crushed peppercorns, sugar, salt and whisky.

3. On a large work surface, lay out a square of double-layered cling film and spread a layer of the cure mixture in the centre, the same size as the salmon fillet. Place the salmon on top, skin side down, then cover with the remaining cure mixture. Wrap the cling film tightly around the salmon, put on a tray and leave in the fridge to cure for 36 hours.

4. Remove the cure from the salmon by gently scraping then washing under a cold tap. Pat the fish dry in a clean tea towel and re-wrap in cling film. Keep in the fridge until you need it, for up to a week.

5. To serve the gravadlax, chop and mix the remaining dill with a tablespoon of olive oil. Rub onto the gravadlax before slicing it thinly like smoked salmon and dividing it between 4 plates with pickled beetroot, creamed horseradish and brown bread.

Prawn Cocktail

Prawn Cocktail

The classic prawn cocktail is a firm festive favourite. The secret is to buy really good quality prawns and to make sure the lettuce is fresh and crisp.

Serves 4   25 mins preparation

Ingredients

400g cooked shell-on prawns

8 tablespoons mayonnaise

2 tablespoons tomato ketchup

1 tablespoon brandy

1 lemon

Salt and milled black pepper

2 dashes Tabasco

2 Little Gem lettuce

¼ cucumber

2 tomatoes

2 spring onions

1 pinch paprika

1. Peel the shells from the prawns, keeping four intact for the garnish. Wash them and leave to dry in a colander.

2. Make a Marie Rose sauce by mixing the mayonnaise, ketchup, brandy, juice of half a lemon, a pinch of salt, a twist of milled black pepper and the Tabasco.

3. Remove and discard the outer leaves of the lettuce. Shred the hearts finely and divide between four dishes.

4. Peel and de-seed the cucumber and tomatoes. Dice into small cubes and again divide between the four dishes.

5. Peel the spring onions, slice them very finely and sprinkle over the lettuce, cucumber and tomatoes.

6. Pile the prawns on top, spoon over the Marie Rose sauce and dust with a little paprika. Add a lemon wedge to each dish and place a whole prawn on top.

Smoked Salmon with Traditional Garnish

This is the tastiest way to serve simple smoked salmon. The tangy garnish and horseradish cream balance the richness of the fish perfectly.

Serves 4   25 mins preparation

Ingredients

100g horseradish sauce

25ml double cream

Juice of 1 lemon

Sea salt

500g smoked salmon, sliced

50g shallots, finely chopped

50g gherkins, finely chopped

50g baby capers

2 hard boiled eggs, grated

1 lemon, cut into wedges

4 slices brown bread and butter

Milled black pepper

1. Mix the horseradish sauce and double cream with 2 tablespoons of lemon juice and a pinch of sea salt. Place in a small dish to serve at the table.

2. Divide the salmon equally between 4 plates. Then arrange the shallots, gherkins, capers and grated egg in 4 separate piles on the edge of the smoked salmon.

3. Serve with lemon wedges, the horseradish cream, brown bread and milled black pepper.

Smoked Salmon with Traditional Garnish

Potato and Aubergine Press with Soft Goats' Cheese

Amongst all the Christmas cooking, it's good to ring the changes by introducing some unexpected flavours. With this starter, the richness of the aubergine is balanced beautifully by the fresh creaminess of goats' cheese – all nicely seasoned with herbs, spices and garlic.

Serves 4   1 hour 30 mins preparation and cooking, 3 hours chilling

Ingredients

2 aubergines

100ml olive oil

1 teaspoon sea salt

1 teaspoon ground cumin

1 clove garlic, thinly sliced

4 sprigs thyme

70ml double cream

140g pasteurised goats' cheese

2 large baking potatoes

Salt and milled black pepper

To serve:

2 cooked beetroot

1 small bunch watercress

4 small baking rings (6.5cm diameter)

1. Preheat the oven to 170°C/gas mark 3.

2. Cut one of the aubergines in half lengthways and score criss-crosses with a knife, deep into the flesh.

3. Place the aubergine, skin side down, on a large sheet of tin foil on top of a baking tray. Drizzle with 2 tablespoons of olive oil and sprinkle with sea salt, ground cumin, garlic and thyme. Wrap and crunch the foil loosely to make a parcel and bake in the oven for 45 minutes.

4. In a saucepan, bring the cream to a simmer, remove from the heat and crumble in the goats' cheese. Use a wooden spoon to beat the mixture vigorously until smooth. Place in a bowl and chill in the fridge.

5. Peel the baking potatoes and cut into 5mm slices. Using one of the baking rings, press out 12 discs from the sliced potatoes. Place these discs in a bowl, add 2 tablespoons of olive oil and sprinkle with salt and milled black pepper. Ensure every disc is well covered with the seasoned oil, then spread them out onto a lined baking sheet.

6. Bake in the oven for 15 minutes, until just tender, then keep in a warm place until you assemble the dish.

Continued on page 44

Potato and Aubergine Press with Soft Goats' Cheese

7. Using a sharp knife, carefully cut the remaining aubergine into 5mm slices.

8. Heat a frying pan, add 2 tablespoons of olive oil and fry the aubergine slices in batches until golden brown on both sides. Remove and drain in a colander over a bowl.

9. When the foil parcel of aubergine is ready, remove it from the oven and check it's fully cooked by using a spoon to ensure it's soft. Leave it to cool until cold enough to handle. Discard the thyme leaves and scoop the aubergine flesh away from the skin and into a saucepan. On a low heat, stirring from time to time, cook until the moisture has evaporated, leaving an aubergine paste.

To assemble the dish:

1. Take one of the baking rings and line the base with a layer of sliced aubergine, followed by half a teaspoon of the aubergine paste, then a slice of potato. Repeat the process, finishing with a layer of aubergine.

2. Wrap in cling film and repeat with the remaining rings.

3. Store on a flat tray and chill in the fridge for at least 3 hours (they will keep for up to 2 days).

To serve:

1. Remove the cling film from each ring, place in the centre of a plate and gently slide the ring off the pressed aubergine.

2. Heat an ice cream scoop (or spoons) in boiling water, then scoop out a rolled spoon shape of goats' cheese mixture and place it on top of the pressed aubergine. Garnish with pieces of beetroot, watercress leaves and a drizzle of olive oil.

Christmas Day roast

It has to be roast turkey and all the trimmings! Here you have everything you need for a classic Christmas spread – including some delicious ideas for vegetarians.

Roast Turkey

Roast Turkey

The secret of the perfect roast turkey is making sure it's properly cooked through, yet still nice and moist. If you follow this recipe, your bird will be succulent and full of flavour.

Serves 10-12 **1 hour 15 mins preparation,
2 hours 30 mins cooking, 35 mins resting**
(cooking times depend on the size of bird – see chart below)

Ingredients

5.5kg fresh whole turkey

½ quantity of Chestnut and Apricot Stuffing
(see recipe on page 52)

150g unsalted butter at room temperature

Salt and milled black pepper

200g streaky bacon

1. Take the turkey out of the fridge 1 hour before it's due to go in the oven.

2. Preheat the oven to 240°C/gas mark 9.

3. To stuff the turkey, with wet hands, loosen the skin at the neck end and push your hand between the skin and flesh towards the breast. Now add the stuffing, but not too tightly, then fold the neck flap under the bird's back and secure with a small skewer.

4. Place the turkey on its back in a large roasting tin. Rub it generously with butter and season with salt and pepper. Layer the bacon, in a criss-cross pattern, over the breast.

5. Double wrap the roasting tin and turkey with cooking foil. Cook for 30 minutes, then reduce the oven temperature to 190°C/gas mark 5 and cook for a further 1½ hours.

6. Remove the tin foil from the turkey and keep to one side. Increase the oven temperature to 220°C/gas mark 7.

7. Remove the bacon from the turkey, and keep warm to serve later. Spoon the cooking juices over the breast to keep it moist. Cook for a final 30 minutes, basting with the juices twice more during this time.

8. After this final cooking period, the turkey should look golden brown all over. If you have a meat thermometer, the temperature should be between 68°C and 70°C as it comes out of the oven. Alternatively use a skewer to pierce the bird to check the juices run clear.

9. Rest the turkey for 5 minutes, then carefully lift it onto a warm serving plate, leaving the juices in the tin. (You'll need these for the gravy – see page 60.)

10. Cover the turkey loosely with the foil you saved and keep in a warm place to rest for up to 30 minutes – or while you finish the rest of your lunch preparations.

For different sized turkeys, use the following guidelines (based on an electric oven):

Weight	Roasting time
4.5kg	2 hours
5.5kg	2 hours 30 minutes
7kg	2 hours 45 minutes
9kg	3 hours 30 minutes

Luxury Nut Roast

Luxury Nut Roast

As a Christmas Day vegetarian option, this looks and smells wonderful. It tastes great too, of course – and goes really well with the festive 'trimmings' everyone else eats with the turkey.

Serves 4   15 mins preparation, 50 mins cooking

Ingredients

250g mixed luxury nuts
20g butter for greasing
1 teaspoon Marmite
1 egg, beaten
50g celery, finely chopped
75g carrot, finely chopped
100g shallots, finely chopped
400g tin chopped tomatoes
50g grated mature Cheddar

50g grated Parmesan
1 heaped tablespoon grated fresh ginger
1 tablespoon fresh thyme, chopped
1 tablespoon fresh sage, chopped
1 tablespoon fresh parsley, chopped
½ lemon – juice and grated zest
Milled black pepper

Loaf tin

1. Preheat the oven to 180°C/gas mark 4.

2. Dry roast the mixed nuts on a baking tray for 10 minutes. Put them into a blender and pulse to grind them to a fine crumb.

3. Grease a loaf tin and line the base with greaseproof paper.

4. Add the Marmite to the beaten egg and whisk until combined.

5. In a large bowl, mix the nuts and all the remaining ingredients, then add the egg and mix well.

6. Place the mixture in the loaf tin and bake for 50 minutes, until firm and golden.

7. Remove from the oven to cool slightly before turning out onto a plate.

Chestnut and Apricot Stuffing

The taste and texture of chestnuts combined with the apricots, herbs and other ingredients, make this the perfect Christmas stuffing. Of course it's designed to go with your roast turkey, but I also love it cold from the fridge the next day!

Serves 8-10   25 mins preparation, 40 mins cooking

Ingredients

1 onion, finely chopped

1 tablespoon vegetable oil

20g fresh sage, finely chopped

10g fresh thyme, finely chopped

20g parsley, finely chopped

100g dried apricots, diced

150g white breadcrumbs

200g sausage meat

100g suet

100g peeled chestnuts (vacuum-packed)

1 egg, beaten

1 lemon – juice and grated zest

Salt and milled black pepper

1. In a small saucepan, gently cook the onion in a tablespoon of vegetable oil for 5-7 minutes, until soft and transparent. Remove from the pan and let it cool completely.

2. Put all the herbs into a large bowl and add the apricots, breadcrumbs, sausage meat and suet.

3. Using your fingers, crumble the chestnuts over the stuffing mix. Add the beaten egg, followed by the cold, cooked onion, lemon zest and juice. Season with salt and pepper.

4. Bind everything together and keep in a covered bowl in the fridge until you need it, for up to 24 hours.

5. Use it to stuff the turkey or cook it separately – by rolling it in greaseproof paper then covering it in a layer of cooking foil and baking in a preheated oven for 40 minutes at 180°C/gas mark 4.

Chestnut and Apricot Stuffing

Cranberry, Port and Orange Sauce

Cranberry, Port and Orange Sauce

For many people, roast turkey simply must have cranberry sauce with it. This recipe, with the added depth of orange and port, beats anything you can buy in a jar.

Serves 8-10 10 mins preparation, 30 mins cooking

Ingredients
100g caster sugar
50ml port
1 orange – juice and grated zest
500g fresh cranberries
2 star anise

1. Dissolve the sugar with the port, orange juice and zest over a medium heat. Add the cranberries and star anise, stir and bring to a simmer.

2. Reduce the heat and let the cranberries burst into a rich sauce. This takes about 25-30 minutes.

3. Taste to check the sweetness and add more sugar if necessary.

4. Remove the star anise.

5. Keep the sauce warm until you're ready to serve it.

Bread Sauce

This traditional accompaniment to turkey should always be deliciously creamy – and this recipe also gives you lots of festive flavour.

Serves 8-10 **10 mins preparation, 15 mins cooking, 1-2 hours infusing**

Ingredients

570ml full-fat milk

1 onion, peeled and chopped

10 cloves

2 bay leaves

6 peppercorns

125g white breadcrumbs

40g unsalted butter

2 tablespoons double cream

Salt and milled black pepper

1. In a saucepan, bring the milk, onion, cloves, bay leaves and peppercorns to a simmer.

2. Remove from the heat, cover with a lid and leave to infuse for 1-2 hours.

3. Strain the milk through a fine sieve and reheat to a simmer. Stir in the breadcrumbs and 20g of the butter and leave on the lowest heat, stirring from time to time.

4. After 15 minutes, the breadcrumbs should have swollen and thickened the sauce. Just before serving, add the remaining butter and cream and beat the sauce with a wooden spoon. Check the seasoning and serve.

Bread Sauce

Pigs in Blankets

Pigs in Blankets

The quirky name still raises a smile – as does the sight of these tasty little treats when you serve them as part of the Christmas Day feast.

Serves 8-10 15 mins preparation, 30 mins cooking

Ingredients
150g dry-cure rindless streaky bacon
300g chipolata pork sausages

1. Cut the bacon in half across the middle.

2. On a sheet of cling film, arrange the bacon pieces side by side, then cover with another piece of cling film.

3. Using a rolling pin, press and roll over the bacon to spread it out.

4. Remove the top layer of cling film, place a chipolata on top of each strip of bacon and roll the bacon around it firmly.

5. Cover and chill in the fridge until you're ready to cook them.

6. To cook, simply add to the roasting turkey for the last half hour of cooking. Or you can roast them separately in a small roasting tin at 200°C/gas mark 6.

Turkey Stock and Gravy

To make the best turkey gravy, you can't beat homemade stock. It's very easy, and you can make it up to two days in advance.

Serves 8-10   10 mins preparation, 2 hours 30 mins cooking

Ingredients

For the stock:

Turkey neck and giblets

2 tablespoons rapeseed oil

1 onion, peeled and roughly diced

2 carrots, peeled and roughly diced

1 stick celery, roughly diced

A few parsley stalks

1 bay leaf

4 peppercorns

For the gravy:

2 heaped tablespoons plain flour

Turkey juices

Salt and milled black pepper

To make the stock:

1. Using a colander, wash the neck and giblets in cold running water. Drain and pat dry with kitchen paper.

2. Heat the rapeseed oil in a large saucepan, add the neck and giblets and stir with a wooden spoon until the meat has browned.

3. Add the vegetables, herbs and peppercorns, cover with cold water and bring to simmering point. Simmer gently for 2 hours, removing any surface fat from time to time.

4. Strain the stock into a clean pan, return to the heat and reduce in volume by half.

5. Leave to cool, then cover and keep in the fridge until you need it, for up to 2 days.

To make the gravy:

1. Reheat the turkey stock to a simmer.

2. When you're roasting your turkey – after removing it from the roasting tin, spoon off any excess fat to leave the dark turkey juices. Add 2 heaped tablespoons of flour and whisk into the juices.

3. When the flour is fully mixed in, whisk in the turkey stock until you have a smooth gravy.

4. Pour the gravy back into the pan and keep it simmering slowly to concentrate the flavour until you're ready to serve it.

5. Check the seasoning, pour into a gravy boat and serve.

Turkey Stock and Gravy

Brussels Sprouts with Chestnuts and Bacon

Brussels Sprouts with Chestnuts and Bacon

The one veg you really can't do without at Christmas is Brussels sprouts –
and this is my favourite way to prepare them.

Serves 8-10   10 mins preparation, 15 mins cooking

Ingredients
150g pancetta, diced
150g peeled chestnuts (vacuum-packed)
750g small, firm Brussels sprouts
(remove bases and withered leaves)
20g unsalted butter
Salt and milled black pepper

1. In a large frying pan, fry the pancetta until crisp and golden, then keep warm.

2. Bring a large pan of salted water to the boil. Add the chestnuts, still in the sealed vacuum
   bag, and cook for 5 minutes to warm through.

3. Remove the bag, open the chestnuts and add to the pan of pancetta.

4. Bring the pan of water back to the boil, add the sprouts and cook for 8-10 minutes.
   Drain in a colander.

5. Add the sprouts to the pancetta and chestnuts, then add the butter and stir around the
   pan until it's melted. Season with black pepper and serve.

Red Cabbage

Red Cabbage

This classic winter side dish is packed with all the flavours that work well with roast turkey. You can also serve it with game, sausages or stews.

Serves 8-10   20 mins preparation, 2 hours cooking

Ingredients

1 large red cabbage

Salt and milled black pepper

450g cooking apples, peeled, cored and diced

300g onions, peeled and finely chopped

¼ teaspoon grated nutmeg

¼ teaspoon ground cloves

¼ teaspoon ground cinnamon

2 tablespoons brown sugar

30g unsalted butter, diced

1 tablespoon redcurrant jelly

3 tablespoons red wine vinegar

1 tablespoon fresh thyme

1. Preheat oven to 170°C/gas mark 3.

2. Remove and discard the outer leaves of the cabbage. Cut the rest of the cabbage into quarters, removing the hard, white stalk from the centre.

3. Shred the cabbage as finely as you can, using a sharp knife or a food processor.

4. In a large casserole dish, arrange a layer of cabbage to cover the base. Season with salt and pepper, and add a layer of apples followed by a layer of onions, then sprinkle with the nutmeg, cloves, cinnamon and sugar. Continue layering until you've included all the cabbage and apples.

5. Add the butter, redcurrant jelly and red wine vinegar and cover with a tight-fitting lid.

6. Cook for 2 hours, stirring once or twice.

7. When the cabbage is cooked, add the thyme and keep in a warm place until you're ready to serve.

Roast Potatoes

What makes these potatoes so crispy and crunchy? It's the goose fat – and that gentle 'fluffing' before you start roasting.

Serves 8-10   10 mins preparation, 1 hour cooking

Ingredients
2kg King Edward potatoes
1 tablespoon salt
150g goose fat

Roasting tin

1. Preheat the oven to 240°C/gas mark 9.

2. Wash and peel the potatoes. Cut each one diagonally to give as much flat surface area as possible. Depending on their size, cut them two or three times, so they're all about the same.

3. Put the potatoes in a large saucepan, cover with water and add half the salt. Bring to the boil and simmer for 5 minutes.

4. Drain the potatoes into a colander, then tip them back into the pan. Put the lid on and shake the pan carefully four or five times to fluff up the edges without breaking the potatoes.

5. Put the goose fat in a roasting tin and heat in the oven for 5 minutes until it's spitting slightly. Carefully add the potatoes and roll them in the fat.

6. Roast for 1 hour, shuffling them in the tin half way through cooking.

7. They should now look crunchy and golden. Remove any excess fat, season with the remaining salt and keep in the oven until you're ready to serve.

Roast Potatoes

Maple Roast Parsnips

These winter root veg have their own sweetness – and roasting them in maple syrup enhances this beautifully.

Serves 8-10   10 mins preparation, 35 mins cooking

Ingredients
1.2kg parsnips
50ml rapeseed oil
25g butter
Salt and milled black pepper
50ml maple syrup

Roasting tin

1. Preheat the oven to 200°C/gas mark 6.

2. Wash and peel the parsnips. Cut lengthways into quarters, removing the white core along the centre.

3. Heat a roasting tin, add the oil and butter and place in the oven for a few minutes until the butter has melted.

4. Add the parsnips, season with salt and pepper and toss them in the melted oil and butter.

5. Roast for 25 minutes, until they've softened and started to brown.

6. Drain off any excess fat, add the maple syrup and coat the parsnips.

7. Put the tin back in the oven and roast for a further 10 minutes.

Maple Roast Parsnips

Dauphinoise Potatoes

Dauphinoise Potatoes

Try these creamy, garlicky potatoes as an alternative to traditional roasties.
Or you could even serve both kinds – it is Christmas, after all.

Serves 4-6   20 mins preparation, 50 mins cooking

Ingredients

500ml whipping cream

2 cloves garlic, finely chopped

¼ teaspoon grated nutmeg

30g butter

1kg King Edward potatoes

1 onion, finely chopped

Salt and milled black pepper

Gratin dish

1. Preheat the oven to 180°C/gas mark 4.

2. Heat the cream and chopped garlic in a saucepan. Bring to a simmer, then remove from
   the heat. Add the grated nutmeg and keep the cream warm.

3. Grease an ovenproof gratin dish with a third of the butter.

4. Wash and peel the potatoes. Slice them thinly, using a mandolin or food processor –
   or use a sharp knife, taking care to keep them a consistent thickness.

5. Place a layer of potatoes in the gratin dish, overlapping their edges. Scatter a thin layer of
   onion, season lightly with salt and pepper, then pour over a ladle of the warm cream.

6. Repeat with three more layers, finishing with a final layer of potatoes.

7. Cut the remaining butter into cubes and scatter over the top.

8. Bake in the oven for 20 minutes, then reduce the heat to 150°C/gas mark 2 and cook
   for a further 30 minutes. Keep warm until you're ready to serve.

Desserts for the perfect finalé

To round off Christmas lunch – and any other festive meal – you might want to offer choices alongside your Christmas pudding. These dishes give you plenty of ideas, from the light and fruity to the rich and creamy.

Caramel Oranges

Sticky sweet caramel, balanced by the citrus burst of fresh oranges. This is an exciting dessert that's not too filling after all the Christmas indulgence.

Serves 4   30 mins preparation and cooking

Ingredients
8 medium-sized seedless oranges
225g caster sugar
150ml cold water
150ml boiling water
2 tablespoons Cointreau (optional)

Cocktail sticks

1. Peel the skin from 4 of the oranges. Remove any pith from the skin with a sharp knife, leaving just the zest.

2. Cut the zest into fine strips and blanch in a small pan of boiling water for 1 minute. Tip into a sieve and rinse with cold water, drain and set aside.

3. Peel all the oranges to the flesh, carefully removing any pith. Slice each one across into 6 circular pieces, then re-assemble using 2 cocktail sticks to keep the slices together. Place the oranges in a serving bowl.

4. Put the caster sugar and cold water into a saucepan and bring slowly to a simmer, shaking the pan gently as the sugar dissolves.

5. Raise the heat and boil rapidly, swirling the pan carefully to dissolve any crystals. Continue to cook until the syrup turns a rich amber colour. This is your caramel.

6. The pan will be very hot – so for the next step, place a pan stand in the bottom of an empty sink and put the pan on top. Now wrap a cloth around your hand and stand well back as you pour the boiling water over the caramel in the pan. Once the spluttering has subsided, stir with a wooden spoon until the mixture is thoroughly blended.

7. Return the pan to the heat. Add the orange zest you prepared earlier and cook for 2 minutes, then pour the caramel over the oranges. Chill in the fridge until you need them, then serve chilled – with the optional Cointreau poured over if you want to give the dish an extra 'kick'.

Caramel Oranges

Baked Alaska

Keeping the ice cream frozen inside the cooked meringue has always seemed like something of a miracle. But if you follow these steps, it works every time – and the flaming kirsch gives this dish an extra 'wow' factor.

Serves 8-10   1 hour 30 mins preparation, 10 mins cooking

Ingredients	For the sponge cake:	For the meringue:
1 Victoria sponge – or make your own (as the recipe, right)	55g unsalted butter at room temperature, plus extra for greasing	6 egg whites
750ml tub of good quality vanilla ice cream	55g caster sugar	1 pinch salt
250g raspberry sorbet	1 egg, beaten	1 teaspoon cream of tartar
600g jar of cherry compote	1 drop vanilla essence	200g caster sugar
50ml kirsch (optional)	55g self-raising flour	
		Piping bag with star nozzle
	16cm round baking tin	Eggcup – to contain the kirsch, if you're including it, so it needs to be ovenproof and flameproof

First, make the sponge cake:

1. Preheat the oven to 190°C/gas mark 5.

2. Grease the baking tin with the extra butter and line the base with greaseproof paper.

3. Using an electric mixer, cream the butter and sugar until pale and fluffy. Slowly add the beaten egg, a little at a time, beating well after each addition.

4. When all the egg is mixed in, add the vanilla essence. Then add the flour, folding one third at a time into the mixture. When you've mixed in all the flour, pour the cake mixture into the baking tin.

5. Bake on the centre shelf of the oven for 25 minutes. When it's cooked, let it rest for 5 minutes, then remove it from the cake tin and put it on a wire rack to cool.

Next, start to assemble the Baked Alaska:

1. When the sponge cake is cool (or if you're using a bought sponge), use a serrated knife to cut carefully through it horizontally, as if you were making a sandwich cake. Keep one half to form the base of the Baked Alaska. (You don't need the other half for this recipe, but you could use it in the Raspberry and Banana Trifle – see page 82.)

2. Place the sponge base in an ovenproof dish, lined with greaseproof paper.

3. Dip the tub of vanilla ice cream in a bowl of hot water for 2 seconds to loosen it. Then tip it carefully onto the sponge, leaving a clear border all the way around.

4. Place the raspberry sorbet on top of the ice cream, creating a mound on top of the sponge base.

5. Put the part-made Alaska in the freezer until firm.

Continued on page 78

Baked Alaska

Make the meringue:

1. Whisk the egg whites until they're foamy, then add the salt and cream of tartar. Continue whisking until soft peaks start to form.

2. Gradually add the caster sugar, beating well after each addition, until you have a thick, glossy meringue mixture.

3. Spoon the mixture into the piping bag.

Then finish assembling the Alaska:

1. Remove the part-made Alaska from the freezer and place the eggcup on top of the raspberry sorbet – upright, for pouring the kirsch into.

2. Pipe the meringue mixture around the Alaska, all the way up the sides of the eggcup, but leaving the bowl of the eggcup clear.

3. Make sure you've covered all the ice cream and sorbet, then put the Alaska back in the freezer until you need it, for up to 3 days.

To cook and serve the Baked Alaska:

1. Preheat the oven to 200°C/gas mark 6.

2. Bake the Alaska for 8-10 minutes, until lightly coloured.

3. Meanwhile, heat the cherry compote in one small saucepan and the kirsch in another.

4. Remove the Baked Alaska from the oven. Pour the hot kirsch carefully into the eggcup, and light with a match. Slice and serve with the warm cherry compote.

Crème Brûlée

Crème Brûlée

This luxurious dessert is a favourite on many restaurant menus, and it's quite easy to make at home. The blowtorch isn't essential, but it's worth getting hold of one if you can, as it gives the crispest caramel topping.

Serves 4   **20 mins preparation, 50 mins cooking, 6 hours chilling**

Ingredients

500ml double cream
1 vanilla pod, split lengthways
6 large egg yolks
4 tablespoons caster sugar

4 ramekin dishes
Blowtorch (or a very hot grill)

1. Preheat the oven to 160°C/gas mark 3.

2. In a saucepan, bring the double cream and vanilla pod to a simmer. Using a whisk, disperse the vanilla seeds from the pod.

3. In a large bowl, whisk the egg yolks with the caster sugar, until well mixed in.

4. Remove the vanilla pod and pour the warm cream onto the egg mixture, stirring vigorously.

5. Divide the egg and cream mixture between the 4 ramekin dishes and put them in a deep-sided baking tray or roasting tin. Pour boiling water around the ramekins to make a water bath, three quarters of the way up the sides of the dishes.

6. Cook in the oven for 45 minutes, then remove the ramekins from the water bath and allow to cool.

7. Chill in the fridge for at least 6 hours – they will keep for up to 2 days.

8. About 1 hour before serving, sprinkle a fine layer of caster sugar over the top of each ramekin, then flame it with a blowtorch until you have a light, crisp caramel. If you don't have a blowtorch, you can use a very hot grill.

Raspberry and Banana Trifle

Raspberry and Banana Trifle

The great British trifle has made a welcome comeback in recent years. Thankfully we're throwing away the packet mixes and going for the real thing – like this one, with proper homemade custard and plenty of whipped fresh cream.

Serves 6   45 mins preparation, 4-12 hours chilling

Ingredients

120g sponge cake (shop-bought sponge fingers are fine, or if you're making the Baked Alaska you could use the leftover sponge, see page 76)

2 tablespoons raspberry jam

2 tablespoons water

35ml sherry

250g raspberries (fresh or frozen)

2 bananas, sliced

200ml double cream

20g toasted flaked almonds

For the custard:

300ml double cream

1 vanilla pod, split lengthways

5 egg yolks

60g caster sugar

1 teaspoon cornflour

1. In a trifle bowl, break the sponge into large pieces, about 5cm square.

2. Put the raspberry jam and water into a small saucepan, and bring to a simmer.

3. When the jam has melted, pour it over the sponge.

4. Sprinkle the sherry over the sponge and jam, and add half the raspberries, then the sliced bananas and then the remaining raspberries.

To make the custard:

1. In a saucepan, bring 300ml of double cream and the vanilla pod to a simmer. Using a whisk, disperse the vanilla seeds from the pod, then remove the pod.

2. In a separate bowl, beat the egg yolks, caster sugar and cornflour. Pour one third of the warm cream over and whisk well before adding the rest.

3. Pour the custard back into the pan and cook very gently over a low heat, stirring all the time until the custard has thickened. (Be very careful at this stage: if you over-heat the custard, the eggs might scramble.)

To finish the trifle:

1. Remove the custard from the heat and whisk it vigorously to disperse the heat. Pour it over the trifle, let it cool and keep it in the fridge for at least 4 hours or overnight.

2. Whip 200ml of double cream into soft peaks. Spread it over the top of the custard and decorate with the toasted almonds.

Poached Pears in Mulled White Wine

Poached Pears in Mulled White Wine

This Christmassy version of poached pears gives you all that festive spice and sweetness in a relatively light dessert. You can use virtually any kind of white wine – but save your best pudding wine to drink with it!

Serves 6   15 mins preparation, 30-40 mins cooking

Ingredients

200ml cider	3 star anise
1 bottle of white wine	50g root ginger (one whole piece)
1 orange – juice and grated zest	4 cloves
1 lemon – juice and grated zest	150g caster sugar
1 cinnamon stick	6 pears

1. In a large saucepan, heat the cider and reduce in volume by half.

2. Add the white wine and bring to a simmer.

3. Add the orange and lemon juice and zest, cinnamon stick, star anise, ginger, cloves and sugar. Simmer for 10 minutes.

4. Peel the pears, leaving the stalks intact. Cut a slice off the bottom of each one, so they can stand upright.

5. Poach the pears gently in the mulled wine for 20 minutes. Pierce them with a sharp knife to check for firmness. If they still feel hard, cook them for a little longer, until they have softened slightly (this depends on how ripe they are).

6. Leave the pears to cool in the mulled wine. Then place them in a suitable bowl and cover with half the mulled wine.

7. Strain the remaining mulled wine into a saucepan and reduce it to a syrup consistency. Leave to cool.

8. To serve, stand each pear on a plate and pour a little syrup over. They go perfectly with vanilla ice cream – or try them with a good blue cheese.

Raspberry Soufflé

Raspberry Soufflé

A fluffy, fruity soufflé is always sure to impress your guests. This one has an extra surprise: a few fresh raspberries hidden in the centre.

Serves 6   35 mins preparation, 10 mins cooking

Ingredients

20g unsalted butter

150g caster sugar, plus about 50g for coating

24 fresh raspberries

60ml framboise (raspberry eau de vie), optional

250ml raspberry purée

10g cornflour

50ml water

6 egg whites

Icing sugar for dusting

6 ramekin dishes

1. Preheat the oven to 180°C/gas mark 4.

2. Grease the ramekins with the butter and sprinkle the extra caster sugar for coating around the dishes so it sticks evenly to the butter. Discard any excess sugar.

3. In a small dish, marinade the raspberries in 40ml of framboise if you're using it. If not, leave the raspberries for later.

4. Sieve the raspberry purée into a pan. Over a medium heat, reduce the volume by half.

5. In another small dish, dissolve the cornflour in 20ml of framboise if you're using it. If not, use 20ml of water. Add to the reduced purée and stir until thickened, then remove from the heat.

6. In a clean pan, mix 50g of the caster sugar with 50ml of water and bring to the boil. Simmer until the temperature reaches 120°C. Add this to the raspberry purée, mixing together. Leave to cool.

7. Whisk the egg whites using an electric mixer. When they start to take shape, begin adding the remaining 100g of caster sugar, a little at a time, whisking after each addition until it's all mixed in.

8. Pour the raspberry purée mixture into a large bowl. Whisk in a third of the beaten egg whites, then carefully fold in the rest to keep it as light as possible.

9. Half fill each ramekin. Place three drained raspberries in the centre, then fill with the remaining soufflé mix.

10. Use a palette knife to press the soufflé mixture into each ramekin and scrape off any excess to leave a smooth flat surface. This is important, to ensure that the soufflés rise evenly. Use a piece of kitchen paper to wipe around the rim of each ramekin.

11. Bake the soufflés for 8-10 minutes, until they're well risen and golden. Serve with a raspberry on top of each one, dusted with sieved icing sugar.

Seasonal main dishes

In many households, Christmas entertaining is more than just one meal. If you need inspiration for several days, here's where you'll find it – whether you favour traditional meat and game, or fancy a change with fish or vegetarian options.

Salmon en Croute

Salmon en Croute

Serves 4   40 mins preparation, 35 mins cooking

Ingredients

250ml milk
½ onion, finely chopped
1 bay leaf
3 cloves
40g unsalted butter
30g plain flour

100g cheddar cheese, grated
4 salmon fillet portions, with
skin and bones removed
Salt and milled black pepper
1 packet filo pastry
100ml white wine

150ml fish stock
50ml double cream
50g cold unsalted butter, diced
Juice of 1 lemon
1 small bunch chives,
finely chopped

1. In a saucepan, bring the milk, onion, bay leaf and cloves to the boil. Remove from the heat and leave to infuse for 10 minutes.

2. In a separate saucepan, over a gentle heat, melt 20g of the unsalted butter. Then add the flour and stir vigorously with a wooden spoon to form a roux (the thickener for your cheese sauce).

3. Continue cooking the roux for a further 2 minutes, stirring continuously.

4. Strain the infused milk and add a little at a time to the roux, stirring until smooth between each addition. Once you've added all the milk, cook on a low heat for a further 10 minutes, stirring regularly.

5. Remove from the heat and beat in the grated cheese. Leave to cool completely.

6. On a chopping board, use a sharp knife to cut a slit in each salmon fillet. Fill each one with a tablespoon of the set sauce and season with a twist of black pepper.

7. In a small saucepan, melt the remaining 20g of butter.

8. On a cool work surface, unwrap a sheet of filo pastry and brush with some of the melted butter. Fold the sheet in two and place one of the salmon fillets on top, then brush around again with the melted butter. Roll and fold the pastry to form a sealed parcel. Repeat with the remaining salmon fillets, then keep in the fridge until you need them.

9. Preheat the oven to 180°C/gas mark 4.

10. Heat a flat baking tray in the oven for 5 minutes, then remove and grease with a little oil. Carefully place each salmon en croute on the tray, brush with a little melted butter and bake for 15 minutes, until golden.

11. Heat the white wine in a saucepan, reducing the volume by half. Add the fish stock and reduce by half again, then add the double cream and simmer. Once the sauce is starting to thicken, turn down the heat and gradually whisk in 50g of cold, diced butter. When it's all mixed in, add the lemon juice and season with salt and pepper to taste.

12. To serve, place each salmon en croute on a warm plate. Reheat the sauce, add the chives and pour immediately onto the plate.

Roast Pheasant with Sage Bread Sauce

This comforting winter warmer packs in loads of concentrated gamey flavours. By adding the pheasant meatballs and red wine sauce, you've got a memorable dish for entertaining.

Serves 2   1 hour 10 mins preparation, 30 mins cooking

Ingredients

1 pheasant (ask your butcher to skin it, detach the legs, take the breast off the bone, and save the carcass for stock)

1 onion, finely chopped

Zest of 1 lemon

1 teaspoon chopped thyme

1 teaspoon chopped parsley

½ teaspoon mustard powder

80g white breadcrumbs

Salt and milled black pepper

1 egg, beaten

8 very thin slices of dry-cure streaky bacon

1 bunch sage leaves

250ml milk

30g unsalted butter

25ml double cream

2 tablespoons rapeseed oil

For the red wine sauce:

Pheasant carcass

½ onion, chopped

1 carrot, peeled and chopped

1 stick celery, chopped

1 bay leaf

A few parsley stalks

250ml red wine

250ml chicken stock

To make the pheasant meatballs:

1. Using a sharp knife, carefully remove as much meat as you can from the pheasant legs. Keep the bones for the stock.

2. Carefully slice the leg meat as finely as possible, then chop thoroughly until it resembles mince.

3. In a bowl, mix the chopped onion, lemon zest, chopped thyme, chopped parsley, mustard powder, pheasant leg mince, 20g of the breadcrumbs and season with salt and pepper. Add the egg and bind into a meaty stuffing, then roll into 4 balls (about golf ball size). Keep in the fridge – you can do this up to 1 day in advance.

To make the red wine sauce:

1. In a large pan, heat the pheasant bones until brown all over. Then add the chopped onion, carrot, celery, bay leaf and parsley stalks. Cook for 2 minutes, then add the red wine. Reduce by half, then add the chicken stock. Bring to the boil and simmer for 40 minutes.

2. Pass through a very fine sieve into a clean pan. Heat and reduce again by half, then let it cool. Keep in the fridge – again, you can do this up to 1 day in advance.

Continued on page 94

Roast Pheasant with Sage Bread Sauce

To prepare the pheasant breasts:

1. Spread out a double sheet of cling film on a work surface and lay 4 slices of bacon on it, in a row. Put 2 sage leaves on top, then a breast of pheasant.

2. Wrap the bacon over the pheasant and roll and wrap it tightly with the cling film. Repeat with the second breast and keep both in the fridge until you need them.

To make the sage bread sauce:

1. Keep 6 sage leaves to one side and put the rest, including the stalks, into a small saucepan. Add the milk and bring to a simmer. Take off the heat, cover and leave to infuse for 30 minutes.

2. Strain the milk and pour into a clean saucepan. Bring it gently back to the boil and stir in the remaining breadcrumbs, 10g of the butter and the cream. Season with salt and pepper, set aside and keep warm until you need it.

To roast and serve the pheasant:

1. Preheat the oven to 180°C/gas mark 4.

2. Heat a large frying pan and add 1 tablespoon of rapeseed oil. When it's smoking, add the 6 sage leaves you saved and fry for 30 seconds until crisp. Remove them from the pan, place on kitchen paper and sprinkle with a little salt.

3. Using the same pan, add the remaining 20g of butter. When it's foaming, add the pheasant breasts (removing the cling film first) and the meatballs. Brown everything all over for 5-10 minutes.

4. Transfer into an ovenproof dish and cook for 20 minutes. Remove from the oven and keep in a warm place.

5. Reheat the red wine sauce and reduce to a syrup consistency.

6. Divide the bread sauce between 2 warmed plates. Carve the pheasant breasts into 4 slices and arrange on the plates along with the pheasant meatballs.

7. Pour the red wine sauce over the pheasant and garnish with the crisp sage leaves.

Game Pie

Game meats and winter vegetables, marinated in wine and herbs and topped with a crisp suet pastry. I can't think of a better way to keep out the December cold.

Serves 6   2 hours 30 mins preparation, 35 mins cooking
12 hours marinating

Ingredients
850g haunch of venison,
cut into 4cm cubes
1 wild duck, cut into 8 pieces
(your butcher will do this for you)
1 pheasant, cut into 8 pieces
(again, your butcher will do
this for you)
100ml rapeseed oil
2 tablespoons tomato purée
50g plain flour
1 tablespoon red currant jelly
Salt and milled black pepper

For the marinade:
15 juniper berries
10 black peppercorns
2 bay leaves
2 sprigs thyme
1 bottle red wine
3 carrots, peeled and
cut into 2cm cubes
3 onions, peeled and
cut into 2cm cubes
3 sticks celery,
cut into 2cm cubes

For the pastry:
225g self-raising flour,
plus extra for dusting
1 teaspoon salt
85g suet
60g butter
150ml water
1 egg, beaten
Sea salt

To serve:
Mashed potatoes
Green vegetables

Large casserole dish   Muslin cloth and string

To marinade the meat and vegetables:

1. Place the juniper berries, peppercorns, bay leaves and thyme in the muslin cloth. Tie firmly with string to make a bouquet garni.

2. Heat the red wine in a large pan, reducing the volume by half. Remove from the heat, add the chopped vegetables, bouquet garni, venison, duck and pheasant.

3. Cover and store in a cool place for 12 hours.

Continued on page 98

Game Pie

To cook the meat and vegetables:

1. Preheat the oven to 120°C/gas mark ½.

2. Strain the marinated meat and vegetables through a colander over a saucepan. Keep the marinade to one side.

3. Pat the meat and vegetables dry with kitchen paper.

4. Heat a large casserole dish, add a little of the rapeseed oil and cook the meat in small batches until browned all over. Keep the meat in a bowl until you need it.

5. Add the tomato purée to the casserole dish and stir into the meat juices for one minute. Add the flour and stir into a smooth paste.

6. Gradually pour over the reserved marinade, stirring all the time.

7. Add the vegetables and cooked game, then enough water to cover the meat. Add the bouquet garni.

8. Bring to a simmer, put a lid on the casserole dish and cook in the oven for 2½ hours.

9. When cooked, the meat should be tender. Remove the bouquet garni, season and mix in the redcurrant jelly. Leave to cool.

To make the pastry:

1. Mix the flour, salt, suet and butter together in a large bowl, until it resembles breadcrumbs.

2. Make a well in the centre and gradually mix in the water to form a smooth dough.

3. Knead for one minute, wrap in cling film and keep in the fridge until you need it.

To assemble and cook the pie:

1. Preheat the oven to 200°C/gas mark 6.

2. When the meat is cool, place it in a large pie dish.

3. On a floured work surface, roll out the pastry to a thickness of 5mm. Cut a thin strip, long enough to go around the edge of the pie dish. Press it onto the dish and brush with beaten egg.

4. Cover the pie with the remaining pastry, sealing the edges together firmly. Brush the top with beaten egg and sprinkle all over with a little sea salt.

5. Using scissors, snip three slits in the centre, then bake in the oven for 35 minutes, until golden brown.

6. Serve with mashed potatoes and green vegetables.

Beef Wellington with Madeira Sauce

Beef Wellington with Madeira Sauce

Classic British dishes always hit the mark at Christmas time – especially when they're a treat like this, with the tender beef fillet, melt-in-the-mouth pastry, and rich pâté and mushroom filling.

Serves 6   1 hour preparation, 35-40 mins cooking

Ingredients

1kg whole centre fillet of beef (Aberdeen Angus if possible)

4 tablespoons rapeseed oil

Salt and milled black pepper

200g shallots, finely chopped

350g button mushrooms, finely chopped

2 sprigs tarragon

1 tablespoon chopped parsley

75g breadcrumbs

80g good quality chicken liver pâté

Flour for rolling the pastry

300g block of puff pastry

1 egg, beaten

2 egg yolks

For the sauce:

100ml Madeira

100ml red wine

200g veal stock

1. Heat a large frying pan until smoking. Meanwhile, take the beef fillet and rub with about 2 tablespoons of the rapeseed oil, then season with salt and pepper. Carefully place into the hot pan and seal the meat until browned all over (about 2 minutes). Remove from the pan, place on a tray to cool, then chill in the fridge.

2. Using the same pan, add the remaining rapeseed oil if required, then gently cook the shallots until soft and transparent. Add the mushrooms, then increase the heat and cook until all the liquid has evaporated. Remove from the heat and let it cool, then add the tarragon, parsley, breadcrumbs and pâté. Season with salt and pepper and mix thoroughly.

3. On a floured work surface, roll out the pastry to a rectangle 3mm thick and brush all over with the beaten egg. Spread the mushroom mix to within 3cm of the edge of the pastry. Place the beef at one end of the pastry and carefully roll it up, making sure the final join is underneath. Gather together the ends and trim off any excess pastry.

4. Place on a tray lined with greaseproof paper and return to the fridge for 30 minutes.

Continued on page 102

To bake the Beef Wellington:

1. Preheat the oven to 190°C/gas mark 5 and warm up a baking sheet.

2. Take the Wellington from the fridge and prick the pastry all over with a fork. Brush with the 2 egg yolks, using a pastry brush.

3. Carefully place the Wellington onto the preheated baking tray and cook in the oven for 35-40 minutes.

To make the sauce:

1. Pour the Madeira into a hot saucepan and reduce the volume by half. Add the red wine and reduce by half again.

2. Add the veal stock, turn down the heat and simmer to a sauce consistency. Keep it warm until you need it.

To serve the Beef Wellington:

1. Once cooked, let the Beef Wellington rest for 5 minutes, before moving it carefully onto a carving board and cutting it into thick slices.

2. Serve with the Madeira sauce.

Mustard and Maple Glazed Ham

For me, poaching and glazing a ham at home is one of the great pleasures of the festive season. The aromas while it's cooking are heavenly, and the flavours are much more complex than in any shop-bought ham.

Serves 18-20 **30 mins preparation, 4 hours 50 mins cooking, 3 hours resting**

Ingredients

For poaching the ham:

6kg gammon on the bone (check with your butcher if it needs soaking)

1 large onion, peeled and halved

1 fennel bulb, halved

1 garlic bulb, halved

3 carrots, peeled and halved

2 sticks celery

3 bay leaves

6 cloves

8 black peppercorns

4 star anise

1 teaspoon fennel seeds

For the glaze:

20 cloves

1 tablespoon ground cinnamon

75g brown sugar

75g English mustard

75g maple syrup

1. Place the gammon in a large pan with the rest of the poaching ingredients. Cover with water, bring to the boil and simmer for 3½ hours, occasionally skimming off any surface sediment. You may need to top up with boiling water from time to time.

2. Leave to cool for 1 hour, leaving the gammon in the liquid.

3. Preheat the oven to 200°C/gas mark 6.

4. Lift the gammon onto a baking tray. Strain the liquid and keep to use as stock in other recipes (it's perfect for pea and ham soup).

5. Using a sharp knife, strip the rind carefully away from the fat. Score a diamond pattern into the fat, with the lines about 2cm apart. Stud the fat with cloves.

6. Mix the ground cinnamon, sugar, mustard and maple syrup together to make the glaze.

7. Line a roasting tin with cooking foil and place the gammon on top. Pour the maple syrup mixture evenly over it and roast for 20 minutes.

8. Remove from the oven and leave to stand for 3 hours before carving.

Mustard and Maple Glazed Ham

Butternut Squash Ravioli with Rocket, Sage and Pine Nut Butter

Butternut Squash Ravioli with Rocket, Sage and Pine Nut Butter

If you're looking for a meat-free option over Christmas, this fresh pasta dish is substantial and tasty enough to please vegetarians and carnivores alike.

Serves 4   **1 hour preparation, 1 hour 30 mins chilling, 5 mins cooking**

Ingredients

For the pasta dough:
300g flour, plus extra for flouring the work surface (00 flour or strong plain flour)
1 pinch salt
2 whole eggs
3 egg yolks
1 tablespoon olive oil

For the filling:
500g butternut squash
150g unsalted butter
1 pinch grated nutmeg
Salt and milled black pepper
2 tablespoons 00 flour (strong plain flour)

For the ravioli:
1 egg, beaten
2 tablespoons olive oil

To serve:
20 sage leaves
50g toasted pine nuts
2 handfuls rocket, washed
½ lemon
100g Parmesan shavings

Pasta machine or rolling pin
7.5cm fluted pastry cutter

To make the pasta dough:

1. Place the flour and salt in a food processor. Using the pulse button, slowly add the eggs and extra yolks, one at a time.

2. When it's all mixed in, add the tablespoon of olive oil.

3. When the oil is mixed in, remove the dough from the machine and knead it for a few minutes on a lightly floured surface.

4. Wrap the dough in cling film and rest it in the fridge for at least an hour.

Continued on page 108

To make the filling:

1. Preheat the oven to 200°C/gas mark 6.

2. Peel, de-seed and dice the butternut squash into evenly sized cubes.

3. Place a square of greaseproof paper (large enough to take the butternut squash) onto a larger square of cooking foil. Put the squash onto the greaseproof paper, add 75g of the butter and sprinkle with the nutmeg, salt and pepper.

4. Lift the foil corners and crunch together to form a sealed parcel (this will steam and roast the butternut squash in its own juices).

5. Cook in the oven for 25 minutes, until tender.

6. Remove from the oven and blend to a fine purée in a food processor. Pour into a bowl and allow to cool.

To make the ravioli:

1. Divide the pasta dough into four. Put one piece through the pasta machine, starting on the widest setting. Keep passing it through on increasingly narrow settings, until you get to the final setting and the pasta is paper thin. (If you don't have a pasta machine, use a rolling pin to roll the pasta as thinly as possible.)

2. Lay the strip of pasta out flat on a floured work surface. Cover with a clean tea towel.

3. Repeat these two steps with a second piece of dough.

4. Spoon about 1 tablespoon of squash filling at 5cm intervals down the length of the first pasta strip. Brush a little beaten egg around each spoonful.

5. Cut the second strip of pasta into equal squares and lay them loosely over each spoonful of filling. Press the top squares down onto the base sheet of pasta to enclose the filling completely, squeezing out any trapped air.

6. Using a 7.5cm fluted pastry cutter, stamp out the raviolis. Lay them out on a floured tray and cover with a clean tea towel.

7. Repeat this process with the remaining pasta and filling.

8. Chill all the filled ravioli in the fridge for at least 30 minutes (up to 24 hours).

To cook and serve the ravioli:

1. Bring a large saucepan of salted water to a simmer. Add 2 tablespoons of olive oil.

2. Add the ravioli and cook gently for 3 minutes. Drain in a colander.

3. Heat a small frying pan and melt the remaining butter until it starts to foam and turn golden.

4. Remove from the heat and add the sage leaves and pine nuts.

5. To serve, divide the pasta between 4 plates. Scatter with the rocket leaves, pour over the sage and pine nut butter, and finish with a squeeze of lemon and the Parmesan shavings.

Making the most of the leftovers

Some of the tastiest dishes are made from leftover food. And they're even better when you know you're not wasting anything. Try these recipes to help you clear out your fridge after Boxing Day.

Bang Bang Turkey

Based on the Chinese dish, Bang Bang Chicken, this fresh, spicy salad is the perfect antidote to the richness of traditional Christmas meals – and a really appetising way to use up leftover turkey.

Serves 4 (or 6 as a starter)   20 mins preparation

Ingredients

4 carrots

6 spring onions

1 cucumber

225g tin of water chestnuts

1 small bunch coriander leaves

500g cooked turkey breast

2 heaped tablespoons smooth peanut butter

20ml sesame seed oil

20ml vegetable oil

30ml soy sauce

2-3 dashes Tabasco

40ml sweet chilli sauce

20g grated fresh ginger (optional)

2 limes

10g toasted sesame seeds

To prepare the salad:

1. Peel the carrots and cut them into very thin strips, like matchsticks.

2. Strip the spring onions of their outer leaves and cut into a similar size.

3. Cut the cucumber in half lengthways, remove the seeds, then cut again like matchsticks.

4. Drain the water chestnuts and slice them thinly. Mix with the carrots, spring onions and cucumber and divide between 4 or 6 plates. Sprinkle with the coriander leaves.

To finish the dish:

1. On a clean chopping board, shred the turkey breast and arrange in equal amounts on the salad plates.

2. Place a heatproof bowl over a pan of simmering water, add the peanut butter and stir with a whisk until it has melted.

3. Remove the pan from the heat but keep the bowl over the water to keep warm. Add the other ingredients, whisking each one in: sesame seed oil, vegetable oil, soy sauce, Tabasco, sweet chilli sauce and optional grated ginger. Whisk until smooth.

4. Squeeze some lime juice over each salad. Spoon the Bang Bang sauce over the turkey and sprinkle with sesame seeds.

Bang Bang Turkey

Turkey and Leek Pie

Turkey and leeks in a creamy white sauce – all topped off with puff pastry. This is my favourite way to make the most of the Christmas bird.

Serves 4   45 mins preparation, 25 mins cooking

Ingredients

250ml chicken stock

250ml milk

30g unsalted butter

50g plain flour, plus extra for dusting

100ml double cream

Salt and milled black pepper

2 leeks

1 tablespoon rapeseed oil

400g cooked turkey leftovers, cut into bite-size pieces

300g puff pastry (ready-made)

1 egg, beaten

1. Preheat the oven to 180°C/gas mark 4.

2. In a saucepan, heat the chicken stock and milk, bring to a simmer, then keep it warm.

3. In a second saucepan, melt the butter, add the flour and use a wooden spoon to stir vigorously to form a roux (the thickener for the white sauce).

4. Continue cooking the roux for a further 2 minutes.

5. Still stirring, add a little of the milk and stock at a time, stirring again after each addition. When you've mixed in all the liquid, cook on a low heat for a further 10 minutes, stirring regularly.

6. Remove from the heat, add the double cream and season with salt and pepper. Leave to cool.

7. Wash the leeks under a running tap. Cut them in half lengthways, then in half again and chop finely.

8. Heat a frying pan and add the rapeseed oil and leeks. Cook for 5 minutes, then add to the white sauce. Fold in the leftover turkey and pour into a pie dish.

9. On a floured work surface, roll out the puff pastry to a thickness of 3mm, ensuring it's more than large enough to cover the dish.

10. Take thin strips of the pastry and place them around the edge of the pie dish. Brush the strips with the beaten egg and place the pastry lid over the pie. Seal the edges by pressing them firmly together.

11. Make 3 slits in the centre of the pastry lid, using scissors. Brush with the remaining egg, and bake for 20-25 minutes.

Turkey and Leek Pie

Turkey Cassoulet

Turkey Cassoulet

In France, this rich, warming bean stew can be made with any kind of meat – often it's goose or duck, and sausages. This festive British version uses up cooked turkey, but feel free to try it with any other leftovers you may have.

Serves 4   15 mins preparation, 40 mins cooking

Ingredients

120g diced pancetta

1 onion, peeled and chopped

2 x 410g tins flageolet beans, drained and washed

400g tin chopped tomatoes

3 cloves garlic, crushed

4 sprigs thyme

600g cooked turkey (leg meat is ideal)

300g chipolata pork sausages

500ml chicken stock

80g white breadcrumbs

1 tablespoon goose fat

1. Preheat the oven to 190°C/gas mark 5.

2. Heat a large casserole dish and add the pancetta. Cook, stirring from time to time, until it starts to crisp.

3. Add the onion and cook for a further 3 minutes, then add the flageolet beans, tomatoes, garlic and thyme.

4. Break the leftover turkey into chunks. Add it to the casserole, along with the chipolata sausages.

5. Add the chicken stock and bring to a simmer.

6. Coat with a layer of breadcrumbs and dot the goose fat around the surface.

7. Bake in the oven for 35-40 minutes.

Broccoli and Stilton Soup

Broccoli and Stilton Soup

If you find you've bought too much Stilton for your festive cheese board, this is a wonderful way to use it up. It makes a substantial starter or tasty lunch, any time up to New Year – and beyond.

Serves 4-6   45 mins preparation and cooking

Ingredients
600g broccoli (about 2 large heads)
20g unsalted butter
1 onion, peeled and diced
1 leek, washed and diced
1 medium potato, peeled and diced
1 litre vegetable stock
150g Stilton, grated
50ml double cream

To serve:
Crusty bread

1. Cut the stalks from the broccoli florets, keeping both to one side.

2. In a large pan, melt the butter, then add the onion and cook it gently for 5 minutes.

3. Add the leek, broccoli stalks and potato. Cook for a further 5 minutes, stirring from time to time. Don't let the vegetables colour.

4. Add the vegetable stock and bring to the boil, then simmer for 15 minutes.

5. Add the broccoli florets and cook for a further 10 minutes.

6. Put the soup in a food processor or liquidiser and blend until very smooth. Pass it through a fine sieve into a clean pan.

7. Using a balloon whisk, stir in the grated Stilton and double cream. Bring the soup back to a gentle simmer, being careful not to let it boil.

8. Serve with lots of fresh crusty bread.

Festive entertaining

Christmas time is party time! In the next few pages, you'll find ideas for canapés, nibbles and everyone's favourite festive cocktails.

Festive Canapés

Smoked Salmon on Rye Canapés

Most people love smoked salmon, and this recipe makes a little go a long way – in a gently spicy style.

Makes 48 canapés   20 mins preparation

Ingredients

½ teaspoon ground cumin

½ teaspoon curry powder

200g soft cream cheese

1 lemon

6 slices of dark rye bread or pumpernickel

200g sliced smoked salmon

1 tablespoon lime pickle

Milled black pepper

1. In a small frying pan on a low heat, dry fry the ground cumin and curry powder for one minute.

2. In a small bowl, mix the cream cheese, toasted spices and the juice of half the lemon.

3. Cut the rye bread into bite-size pieces. Spread each piece with a thick layer of the cream cheese mixture, then top with a twist of smoked salmon and a dot of lime pickle.

4. Finish with milled black pepper and a squeeze of lemon.

Roast Tomato and Mozzarella Tartlets

Ready-made canapé tartlets give you an instant pastry case for your homemade filling and topping. The Italian-inspired flavours here are tried and tested crowd-pleasers.

Makes 24 tartlets   30 mins preparation

Ingredients
400g vine cherry tomatoes
1 teaspoon caster sugar
1 teaspoon sea salt
1 clove garlic, thinly sliced
1 small pinch paprika
2 tablespoons olive oil
24 canapé tartlets
24 mini mozzarella balls
4 basil leaves

1. Preheat the oven to 180°C/gas mark 4.

2. Place the vine tomatoes, with the vines attached, on a small roasting tray. Sprinkle with the sugar, salt, garlic, paprika and olive oil. Roast for 15 minutes.

3. Remove from the oven and cool for a few minutes, until you can handle them. Remove the skins and take the tomatoes off the vines.

4. Put them in a small frying pan, along with any roasting juices. Gently crush them with a fork and cook over a medium heat for a few minutes, to reduce them to a paste-like consistency.

5. Warm the tartlets in the oven for 5 minutes. Fill each one with a teaspoon of the tomato filling and top with a mini mozzarella ball. Sprinkle with torn basil leaves before serving.

Sticky Cocktail Sausages

These variations on honey-and-mustard sausages are popular with party-goers of all ages. They really are sticky though – so give your guests plenty of cocktail sticks.

Serves 20   5 mins preparation, 25 mins cooking

Ingredients

500g cocktail sausages

75g maple syrup

75g Pommery or wholegrain mustard

1. Preheat the oven to 220°C/gas mark 7.

2. Roast the sausages in a roasting tin for 15-20 minutes, shuffling them from time to time so they cook evenly.

3. Mix the maple syrup and mustard together. Pour this over the sausages, using a spoon to coat them.

4. Cook for a further 5 minutes, until they are browned and sticky. Serve warm.

Bloody Mary Serves 1

Ingredients

50ml vodka

60ml tomato juice

1 teaspoon orange juice

1 pinch celery salt

1 pinch black pepper

2 drops Worcestershire sauce

2 drops Tabasco sauce

1 small piece of celery

1. Shake all the ingredients in a cocktail shaker.

2. Strain into a large cocktail glass filled with ice and garnish with the piece of celery.

Buck's Fizz Serves 6-8

Ingredients

4 oranges

1 bottle of Champagne or sparkling wine, well chilled

1. Squeeze the oranges and pass the juice through a fine sieve.

2. Pour the orange juice first – around a third of a glass. Then top up with Champagne or sparkling wine.

Hot Toddy Serves 1

Ingredients

50ml Scotch whisky

2 teaspoons lemon juice

1 tablespoon honey

1 clove

100ml boiling water

1. Put the whisky, lemon juice, honey and clove in a heat-proof glass.

2. Pour over the boiling water, and stir until the honey has melted.

Mulled Wine Serves 8-10

Ingredients

1 bottle of full-bodied red wine
(an Australian or Chilean
Cabernet Sauvignon is ideal)

400ml water

75g caster sugar

100ml port or 75ml brandy

2 oranges, finely sliced

1 lemon, finely sliced

2 cinnamon sticks

2 star anise

2 bay leaves

4 cloves

30g grated fresh ginger

1. Place all the ingredients in a stainless steel saucepan. Bring to the boil and simmer for 15 minutes.

2. Serve hot in heat-proof glasses, preferably with handles.

Festive Drinks

Christmas wines made simple

Christmas wines made simple...

Enjoying food and wine together is one of life's greatest pleasures, but matching the two can seem daunting. Reassuringly, most wines can be enjoyed with most foods, it's all a matter of personal taste.

I have put together a few suggestions to get you started:

Food	Wine	Region
Beef	Cabernet Sauvignon/Merlot	Bordeaux
	Syrah	Northern Rhone
Light Game (i.e. Pheasant)	Pinot Noir	Burgundy and New World
Rich Game (i.e. Venison)	Merlot	Old and New World
	Zinfandel	Old and New World
Pork	Rioja	Spain
	Syrah Shiraz	Old and New World
Chicken, Duck and Turkey	Merlot	Old and New World
	Pinot Noir	Old and New World
Hearty Rustic Dishes (i.e. Game Pie, Cassoulet)	Grenache	Rhone
	Syrah Shiraz	Old and New World
Smoked Salmon	Chardonnay	Old and New World
	Riesling	Old and New World
Shellfish	Muscadet	Loire
	Sauvignon Blanc	Old and New World
Seafood	Albarino	Spain
	Chablis	Burgundy
	Chardonnay	Old and New World
Pasta, Vegetarian (i.e. Luxury Nut Roast, Butternut Squash Ravioli)	Chablis	Burgundy
	Muscadet	Loire
	Chardonnay	New World
	Sauvignon Blanc	New World
Desserts (i.e. Poached Pears, Raspberry and Banana Trifle)	Sweet Riesling	Old and New World
	Tokaj Aszu	New World
Christmas Cake	Muscat	Old and New World

*Old World wines are from Europe, New World wines are from North & South America, South Africa, Australia and New Zealand.

Lamona Appliance, Sink and Tap Collection

The Lamona range is exclusive to Howdens Joinery and has been selected to perfectly complement our range of kitchens.

Lamona appliances are designed to look great and are manufactured to the highest standards to ensure they are durable and reliable, use less energy and water, and run quietly, whilst providing excellent value for money.

You can choose from ovens, microwaves, hobs, extractors, fridges, freezers, dishwashers, washing machines, tumble dryers, sinks and taps, which are all designed to fit beautifully in your Howdens kitchen.

All Lamona appliances come with a 2 year manufacturer's guarantee and what we believe is the best after sales service in the UK.

You will have the reassurance that we supply 500,000 appliances and 600,000 sinks and taps each year to UK homes.

Lamona is available from stock in 500 local depots to your trade professional. To find out more and for detailed product specifications, please refer to **www.lamona.co.uk**

 HOWDENS JOINERY CO. | MAKING SPACE MORE VALUABLE

LAMONA
Exclusive to Howdens Joinery Co.

The General Tarleton

An old coaching inn with contemporary comforts, The General Tarleton Inn is in the pretty village of Ferrensby close to both York and Harrogate. Owned and run by John and Claire Topham for the past 12 years, The General Tarleton is constantly evolving but always sticks to the basic philosophy of offering great service and excellent food and drink in a relaxed atmosphere, and if you are staying the night, a comfortable room to rest your head.

The focus is on food

In The General Tarleton kitchen, John heads an experienced and dedicated team. Menus change daily to reflect the seasons and the pick of the catch or crop that day. John gets a call most days from the fishing boats as they return to port and within hours the fish is in the kitchen. Yorkshire has an abundance of excellent suppliers which The General Tarleton has worked with over the years to obtain the very best seasonal produce.

The General Tarleton Inn, Boroughbridge Road, Ferrensby, Knaresborough, HG5 0PZ
Tel 01423 340284 www.generaltarleton.co.uk